MW01493784

Marbella Travel Guide

Attractions, Eating, Drinking, Shopping & Places To Stay

Steve Jonas

Table of Contents

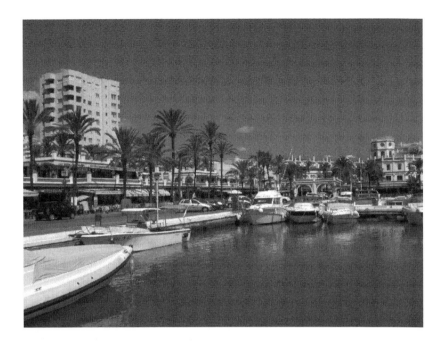

Marbella

Marbella on the Costa del Sol in Spain is the destination of choice for the rich and famous. In Marbella and its neighbour Puerto Banús you will rub shoulders with international celebrities at the super-smart beach clubs and can dance until dawn at the areas famous nightspots.

Marbella and Puerto Banús are linked by the five kilometre Avenida Bulevar Príncipe Alfonso de Hohenlohe, locally known as the Golden Mile. There are several five star luxury hotels with their luxurious tropical gardens that reach down to the sea and their private beach clubs. Halfway along the Golden Mile (set back a few hundred metres) is the Royal Palace of King Fahd. The late king of Saudi Arabia used to come to his palace every year until his death in 2005 bringing a very welcome injection of millions of euros into the local area.

Marbella itself has two distinct parts; the newer area stretches down to the port and marina which in turn leads into the wide promenade. There are many bars and shops in this area along the seafront which faces the flat, sandy beach. On the beach there are plenty of sunbeds and thatched sun umbrellas to hire for a day's relaxation in the sun. The Old Town sits further back up a slight hill and is typically Spanish with plazas, one way streets and dead ends. It is much easier to walk round the Old Town than to drive.

A Spanish ambience remains in Marbella despite the many hotels, restaurants and shops that cater to foreign visitors. It is still possible to find a coffee or beer and a snack for a couple of euros if you look in the right places, but if you want to pay a week's salary for an evenings entertainment you can find that as well.

The main street of Marbella sees expensive sports cars pass through all day long, but in the middle of all this pristine bodywork and glass are wizened Spanish men winding their way through the traffic on old, dusty mopeds. Designer boutiques with guards on the door sit side by side with euro bazaars and mini-markets where señoras dressed in black (as well as tourists) poke though the goods looking for the best buys.

The town itself and the outskirts of Marbella have become home to many clinics where it is not just the stars that come for plastic surgery treatments to enhance their looks. Many health tourists come for facelifts, nose and boob jobs and other processes that try to turn back the clock. And there's no better place to recuperate than in the warm Spanish sun.

Marbella has an established cultural schedule, mainly in the summer but for most of the year there is an event happening somewhere round the town. In addition to concerts there are exhibitions, recitals and readings. There is always a big music choice from opera to jazz and reggae to classical, all manner of tribute bands play to packed audiences as well as some of today's stars performing in person. Some events are in small exclusive venues and others are in places like the local bullring that holds thousands of people. One thing they have in common though especially in the summer is the promise of listening to good music and dancing under a blanket of stars in the warmth of a Mediterranean evening.

Marbella Fair (Feria de San Bernabe) is held in June every year when the streets of the Old Town are lined with stalls while just outside the town a huge fairground with death-defying rides and ear-shattering music goes on until the early hours of the morning. It is a great opportunity to dress up and mingle with the crowds as families, friends and sweethearts come together to take part in one of the party highlights of the year. Several events take place in the days leading up to the fair with processions of horses, floats and people parading through the town. There are fireworks and dancing, marching bands and lots of eating and drinking which all blend together to make a visit to the fair in Spain one to remember.

Planning Your Stay

The Costa del Sol is located in southern Spain in the province of Málaga in the self-governing community of Andalucia. The Costa del Sol spans 160 kilometres from Nerja to Manilva with Marbella in the western-third. Marbella is situated on the Mediterranean Sea and sits under the watchful eye of La Concha, which stands at 1,215 metres high and is part of the Sierra Blanca range of mountains.

The municipality of Marbella extends along the coast for 44 kilometres and has a population of 140,000 permanent inhabitants. It is a transient town though with people of all nationalities passing through every week. Some stay a while and find temporary work, earn a few euros and then move on; others make Spain their home and stay forever.

The lifeblood of many businesses depends on the international tourists that visit Marbella to visit the playgrounds of the wealthy and to enjoy the wonderful climate. Through the peak summer months of July, August and September around one million overnight stays are recorded in Marbella every year.

The closest airport to Marbella is Málaga International Airport approximately 60 kilometres away to the east. Budget flights from all over Europe arrive in Málaga bringing in millions of visitors every year. A multi-million euro expansion plan and second runway in recent years means that Málaga Airport is ready to receive even more travellers in the future.

To get to Marbella from Malaga airport means hiring a car (typically super cheap from about €15/day) or taking a bus or taxi. There isn't a train station in Marbella, the nearest one is in Fuengirola 20 kilometres away and that is only a local line, although it does stop at the airport. There is a direct coach link between Málaga and Marbella which uses the toll road and it is quick and easy. Other bus routes go along the coast road with many stops and are usually quite crowded in the peak months.

Road links are good with the new Málaga bypass meaning anyone driving down from the north of Spain doesn't have to battle through Málaga city centre traffic to get to Marbella. The old coast road runs the length of the Costa Del Sol and although it is a dual carriageway it can get very crowded and is better avoided unless absolutely necessary.

Climate & Weather

Marbella has a Mediterranean climate that is usually mild with dry, hot summers and moderate winters although the peaks of the Sierra Blanca do get a dusting of snow from time to time. The same peaks protect Marbella from icy cold weather blowing in through the winter months and this gives the town a very pleasant micro-climate.

Spring and autumn are the nicest seasons to visit if a hectic sightseeing schedule is on your agenda. The weather is pleasant but not too hot and of course everywhere is slightly less crowded than in the peak summer months. The temperature can reach highs of 24°C in both seasons and dip down to a low of 11°C at night. It can rain in spring and autumn but more often than not it will be a short, heavy downpour.

Summer is hot, hot, hot! The forecast will give a high of 30°C but in reality in direct sun the mercury can reach 40°C and above. The sand can be blisteringly hot so always remember to wear sandals to the beach and wherever you go take lots of high factor sun cream and plenty of water to drink. The locals are easy to spot in the summer, while visitors cook their sun-starved skin to a nice shade of lobster-red the residents walk on the shady side of the street and always sit under umbrellas at the bars. They always looked relaxed in the heat and have no nasty strap marks or giveaway peeling shoulders!

In Spain summer officially starts on the night of San Juan, the 23rd June - 24th June. On beaches everywhere bonfires are lit and families and friends gather together to eat, drink and make merry all night to welcome in another scorching summer. At midnight tradition says you should jump over the bonfire three times to burn away your problems and then run into the sea to cleanse the spirit.

As autumn moves into winter the Spanish people bring out their fur coats, thick jumpers and scarves which makes you think it is really cold. Even in December the high can be around 16° C although nights can be quite nippy and temperatures drop to around 7°C. The winter sun is still pleasant and in a sheltered spot in the middle of the day it can still be warm enough not to need a jumper.

The micro-climate in the area means that Marbella has 320 days of sunshine per year, with 11 hours a day in the summer and about half that figure in winter.

Sightseeing

Selwo Adventure Safari Park

A7 highway km 162, 5
Estepona
29680 Málaga
Tel: +34 952 57 77 73
www.selwo.es/

Selwo Adventure Safari Park is a great day out for all the
family. The park is well designed and you get a real feel
of being out in the wild.

To enter and leave the different territories you pass through enormous wooden gates into the Canyon of the Birds. This is a vast area enclosed by almost invisible netting where the birds fly free among tropical plants and trees and the water sprays give the sense of a steamy jungle.

Cross over the Bridge of Africa and you can get a bird's eye view of the park. The rope and wood bridge sways gently as you cross over high above the lake, 100 metres below. Spread out below are over 2,000 animals from all five continents and there are opportunities to see many of them close at hand by taking the safari tour in the zebra-striped all-terrain trucks. From vantage points on the way round you can see the animals living as they would in the wild. There are no cages and no obvious fencing which gives a real safari feel to the tour.

If you get hungry there is the Fast Food Korongo Restaurant and the Lake Kiosk where energy reserves can be replenished. For a really special night under the stars there are 23 well-appointed cabins at the Selwo Lodge Hotel where you fall sleep listening to the sounds of the wild animals.

The park is open from 10am until about 6pm and later in the summer holidays. In the winter months the park is closed on some days so check before you go. There is an excellent day-to-day calendar on the website. Admission proices are €24.50 adult and €17 for children and OAP's. There are online discounts and various family packages available.

Museum of Contemporary Spanish Engraving

Calle Hospital de Bazán
Marbella
29601 Málaga
Tel: +34 952 76 57 41
www.mgec.es/

The Museum of Contemporary Spanish Engraving opened in 1992 after a donation of 1,350 works by two Spanish authors. Marbella Town Hall gave permission to use the old Hospital Bazán with its Renaissance architecture to house the collection and there are now around 4,000 works in the museum. Prestigious names such as Picasso, Conongar, Miró, Barceló, Tàpies and Caruso are just a few that can be found representing this type of Spanish art. There also many temporary exhibitions and music and art related activities.

The museum is open on Mondays 10am to 2pm, Tuesdays to Fridays 10am to 2.30pm and 5pm to 8.30pm and Saturdays 10am to 2pm. In summer the museum stays open until 10pm Tuesdays to Fridays.

Puerto Banús & Marina

Nueva Andalucía
29660 Málaga

A few kilometres southwest of Marbella is the town of Puerto Banús with its swishy apartments and houses, chic hotels and a 915-berth marina.

The marina was the brainchild of José Banús, a local developer, and designed by Noldi Schreck who was in part responsible for the design of Beverly Hills. The marina complex opened in May 1970 and 1700 guests got through 22 kilos of beluga caviar.

The guest list for the opening was star-studded with Prince Rainier and Princess Grace of Monaco, Hugh Hefner, the Aga Khan and Dr Christiaan Barnard being just a few of the attendees. They were entertained by a very young Julio Iglesias who got the princely sum of 125 thousand pesetas for his performance. Iglesias probably never dreamed that years later he would be one of Spain's biggest stars and have a luxurious home in the hills overlooking that same marina.

The town is the place to see and be seen, international celebrities and the world's jet set flock here in the summer months and the waterfront parking spaces are full of Lamborghini's, Porches and Ferrari's. The multi-million pound yachts and cruisers bob gently up and down with their smartly uniformed staff polishing and cleaning every surface waiting for their wealthy owners to return.

The marina is surrounded by apartments built in typical Mediterranean style and is laid out like a small village with cobbled streets full of designer shops and expensive restaurants. Armed guards stand at the doors of the most exclusive jewellers and car showrooms keeping a watchful eye on anyone that enters.

Across the main coast road from Puerto Banús is Nueva Andalucía and on a Saturday morning this is where the market is held in and around Centro Plaza and the bullring. Old and new, bargains and the not so cheap can all be found here. Clothes, shoes, furniture, bric-a-brac and a good selection of junk are the order of the day along with fruits, vegetables and plants. Trading usually starts about 9am through to 2pm.

Another one of Spain's well known son's is Salvador Dali and it is Dali that created the three ton rhinoceros statue that stands on one on the town's roundabouts. Dali made the sculpture in 1956 for one of his films and in 2004 it was given pride of place in Puerto Banús.

Júzcar Smurf Village

Serrania de Ronda, 29642 Málaga
Tel: +34 952 18 35 67
www.júzcar.es/

Picturesque Spanish mountain villages in the Ronda area usually have white-washed houses nestling against a backdrop of forest.

Not this one as Sony Pictures came to visit in 2011 and painted the whole town blue for the premiere of the Smurfs 3D film. Using 4,000 litres of paint everything in the village was painted Smurf colour, right down to the church and the gravestones. Sony did offer to repaint the village white but the inhabitants voted to keep the colour and visitor figures leapt from just 300 annually to 80,000 in the six months following the film's release.

Even without the pretty shade of blue Júzcar would be an attractive village. Situated inland about 40 kilometres from Marbella the drive takes you up the winding mountain road and into the Serrania de Ronda. The scenery is spectacular with mountains all around and small waterfalls cascading down by the edge of the road.

Júzcar village is quaint with steep streets and oddly shaped chimneys sticking up from ancient rooftops and the most unique building in the village is the 16th century Church of Saint Catherine. There is an ancient Tin Factory to visit and many beautifully crafted items to buy made from hemp and locally grown cork. Stay a while and have lunch in one of the little restaurants; the rabbit cooked with loads of garlic is a speciality of the area.

Marbella Old Town & Orange Tree Square

The pedestrianised cobbled streets of Marbella's Old Town are in complete contrast to the four lane main artery of Avenida Ricardo Soriano just a few hundred metres away. The Old Town of Marbella includes the ancient city walls and the layout of the city is almost the same as in the 16th century. There are intriguing little shops selling a mixture of everyday necessities, locally made goods and luxury items.

Every corner reveals another intriguing passageway or square to admire, some of which are very tiny. Orange Tree Square is the place to head to and this is where the Tourist Office is situated with some very nice bars and restaurants just waiting to be visited. The square has historical buildings on three sides comprising the town hall, the Mayor's house and the Chapel of Santiago.

To the side of the Old Town make a point of finding Calle Rio and Calle San Cristobal. The streets are so narrow that you can stand in the middle and touch the houses on both sides with outstretched arms. The residents here have an amazing display of plants and flowers that fill the street and balconies with every shade of green and a profusion of brightly coloured blooms.

Church of Our Lady

Plaza de la Iglesia
Marbella
29601Málaga
Tel: +34 952 77 31 36
www.diocesismalaga.es/

Close to Orange Tree Square in the Old Town in Marbella is the Church of Our Lady of the Incarnation. This is a popular visitor spot in the Old Town and dates back to 1485 when the Catholic Kings re-conquered Marbella. The church was constructed in 1505 and one its most striking features is the bell tower, reaching up to a height to around 33 metres. The tower has four sections with clocks and bells and the oldest bell is on the east, all this is topped by a pyramid shaped tiled spire. The church is open from 8pm to 10pm for observation and prayer.

Ronda & Tajo Gorge

Ronda 29400
Tel: +34 952 18 71 19
www.turismoderonda.es/

The town of Ronda is about 60 kilometres inland from Marbella and Puerto Banús.

The road up is excellent although winding and there are several restaurants on the way plus various stopping points to take some super photos. Ronda is at an altitude of between 600-700 metres high in the Serrania de Ronda and in winter can get completely cut off by snow. As you climb higher there are snow warning signs at the side of the road, which always seems bizarre in the summer heat.

Ronda is a pretty town with a lot of history behind it. Park on the edge of the town and walk through the narrow streets towards the famous Tajo Gorge and the Bull Ring. It is one of the oldest cities in Spain and archaeological findings put the first signs of civilisation somewhere in the Neolithic age. There is so much to do and see in Ronda it is almost impossible to list. The Tourist Office is opposite the Bull Ring and is the best place to start. Guided tours of the city are on offer or if you prefer to go at your own pace, there is a discounted Visitors Pass. This gives entry into some of the most popular attractions including the Visitor Centre at the Tajo Gorge, two museums and the Arab Baths.

The Bull Ring in Ronda is one of the biggest and most monumental in Spain. The building of the Bull Ring took six years and the fighting arena has a diameter of 66 metres. The two tiers of seating are under 68 archways held up by 136 Tuscany columns and despite the purpose of the structure there is a definite beauty and grace to it. Inside there is a small museum dedicated to bull fighting and a collection of old military weapons.

Tajo Gorge

The view from the Puento Nuevo (New Bridge) over the
Gorge is stunning and you can walk all the way round the
edge admiring the rolling countryside stretching away
towards the mountains from different angles. The bridge
took 42 years to build and from the start of construction in
1751 there were 50 builders who died during the process.
The bridge is 120 metres high and has been used for
various purposes including a prison over the years and
the central arch conceals a chamber that was used as
torture chamber during the Civil War. It is said that
soldiers on both sides of the war threw captured
opponents from the chamber to their death on the rocks
below. There is an exhibition that is open to the public in
the chamber telling the story of the history and
construction of the bridge.

Grazalema & Ubrique Villages

Marbella and Puerto Banús are the most well known
destinations on this part of the Costa del Sol, but spare a
thought for some of the wonderful inland destinations.

There are lots of pretty villages nestled in the mountains
that shelter the coast and it really is worth spending a day
or two exploring. To get to Grazalema head inland
towards Ronda but miss out the town and take the
Algodonales road and then turn off towards Grazalema.

Depending on the time of year there could be vast fields of sunflowers, their smiley yellow faces following the sun all day long. The drive takes you through some of the cork forests and this part of Andalucia is one of the world's biggest producers of cork. It takes nine years for the bark to grow thick enough to be harvested and you can see many different stages of cork growth in the trees as you drive past. Somewhere in the vast forest cork is always being cut as there enough trees for it to be an on-going business on a nine year cycle.

Grazalema

This is only a small village with around 2000 inhabitants but it is incredibly popular with tourists and artists. Many painters come and stay here to take advantage of the clear, natural light and wonderful views. Park in the car park at the far end of the village and admire the view from the lookout point. From this vantage point the view stretches for mile after mile back down towards the coast. A walk down into the village will take you past tiny village houses, their front patios full of brightly coloured geraniums and glossy green plants. There is a small tourist office and several shops selling a variety of daily items and souvenirs.

In the central square there are restaurants whose tables and chairs are all side by side under shady umbrellas and canopies, just right for enjoying an ice-cold beer underneath. Try some of the specialties like oxtail stew, black pudding made with rice or deep fried aubergine crisps drizzled with honey.

To get to Ubrique leave Grazelema behind you but don't go back towards Ronda. Take the road to Villaluenga del Rosario, onwards to Benoacaz and down the hairpin bends into Ubrique. The village of Villaluenga is tiny but there are several factory shops selling goat and sheep cheese and other related products.

Ubrique

The town of Ubrique is perched on a steep hillside and is famous for its amount of leather factories and shops. The population is around 17,000 and many of these people work in leather related industries of which there are over three hundred. It was the Romans who founded Ubrique and started the history of leather making in this pretty Spanish village. The village of Ubrique is now known world-wide as a location for top quality leather goods and many designers seek out the small factories to make their very expensive bags and other goods.

There is a small Leather Museum on Avenida de Herrera Oria where leather working machinery can be seen and a guided tour be taken. The walls are hung with works of art, not painted but make of tooled leather. There are some superb examples of leather goods to see as well as displays of how leather is made into bags. Admission is free but a small donation to the upkeep of the museum is always welcome.

The small church of San Antonio is worth visiting with its pretty belfry and Baroque style. Behind the church is a lookout point which gives an excellent panoramic view of the town and countryside below. Wander back down through the maze of streets and you will be spoilt for choice at the amount of shops to choose from and the beautiful goods on display. The main street is the pretty tree-lined Avenida de España, some of which is traffic free. There are dozens of bars and restaurants scattered along here and all throughout the town where a wide choice of Spanish food to suit all tastes and budgets is available.

Constitution Park

Avenida de la Fontanilla
Marbella
29601 Málaga

Join the locals and take a walk through this Moroccan style park. Constitution Park is only a few minutes away from the Marbella promenade but offers a welcome respite from the searing sun that beats relentlessly down on the sea front. It is an oasis of calm and tranquility which makes it hard to believe that not far away the chaos of Spanish life goes on as usual. It is a great place to for children and there is a well-designed playground as well as an ice-cream parlour. There is a small open air auditorium and through the summer months there are many concerts and exhibitions held in the park

In the summer from about 8pm onwards the park will fill up with extended families bringing their children out to let off steam as the day cools down. With a three month school holiday there is no such thing as bedtime and even the babies and toddlers will still be out until the early hours. The park is beautifully kept and the fir trees soar above the beds of seasonal plants that bring colour to the park all the year round.

Bonsai Museum

Avenida del Doctor Maiz Vinals
Parque Arroyo de la Represa
29600 Marbella
Málaga
Tel: +34 952 86 29 26

The Bonsai Museum in Marbella was created by Miguel Angel Garcia and he still lovingly tends to his miniature trees on a daily basis including the Acebuche Olive which is a mere 300 years young. The collection is known as one of the finest of its kind in the world and some of the other specimens are over 500 years old. The museum is set partly over a lake and turtles can be seen basking lazily in the water below waiting for any bread that might come their way. There is a feeling of calm inside the museum with the sound of the water trickling over the rocks that were specially brought in from nearby El Torcal Country Park in Antequera. For a peaceful retreat from the strong Spanish sun it is worth a stroll up the slight hill to admire these dwarf plants and trees.

Opening hours are 10.30 to 1.30 all year round and 4pm to 7pm. From the middle of July to the end of August it is 5pm to 8.30pm.Admission fee is €4 per adult and €2 for children.

Horse & Carriage Tour

Alameda Park
29601 Marbella
Málaga

A lovely way to see the main attractions in the town of Marbella is to take a gentle ride in a horse and carriage and right next to the Alameda Park there is an equine taxi rank. These beautifully kept animals will take you around the town accompanied by the jingle of harness and the clip clop of hooves which is a lovely relaxed way to travel. Tours last for one hour or 30 minutes and cost around €40 or €20 respectively. The routes can vary but the tour takes in the beaches, the historic Old Town and the centre of the new town, Marbella Castle and Los Lagos amongst other sites.

Estepona

Estepona is virtually surrounded by the Sierra Bermeja massif which is near nearly 1500 metres at its highest point. The rocks have a reddish tinge and this comes from periodite, an igneous rock. This area is the largest mass of periodite found in southern Europe as well as being home to the only forest of Spanish firs found on this type of rock.

This backdrop to Estepona town is stunning, with thick forests of deep green fir trees carpeting the Sierra Bermeja, hiding white villages and picturesque places to stop and admire the view from. From the highest points there are magnificent views across to North Africa and the Atlas and Rif mountains. Lower down towards the sea there are orchards of citrus fruit, meadows for grazing and then areas of scrubland where the land meets the sea.

The Playa de Rada, which won a prestigious EC blueflag in 2009 stretches for around 2.5 kilometres from the giant Carrefour superstore at the eastern end to the pretty little marina at the other. The beach itself is wide, flat and sandy with a beautiful promenade all the way along that is just right for a gentle stroll. The main coastal road divides the beach from the town but thanks to the new toll road the amount of traffic is far less than it used to be. Once across the road the first three streets of the town are parallel to the beach and some are traffic-free. There are many bars and restaurants in this area serving a mixture of traditional and international food and drink. Behind these streets is a maze of smaller, narrow streets hiding a wealth of small shops and boutiques.

The town centre is quite small but there are many urbanisations stretching out to each side and up the slopes behind the town. There is everything here for a super Spanish holiday without quite as much frenetic hustle and bustle of the more popular resorts closer to Málaga.

At the western end of the town is Estepona Marina where there are lots of tapas bars and restaurants', parking is easy as there is a car park at the end of the marina. Estepona town is not really known for its night life but there are several bars and clubs in the marina that stay open until the small hours and play very loud music. The marina is pretty and in the evening when the suns sinks over the horizon and the lights come on it is a pleasant place for a leisurely meal.

For history lovers the church of Los Remedios in Plaza San Francisco in Estepona is worth visiting, built in the 18th century the church has been used as a monastery and as a hospice over the years. Local sandstone was used to build the church which is rich in iron ore and the pieces of iron are easily visible in the walls as you walk around the exterior. The entrance doorway is impressive with a particularly attractive statue of the Virgin Mary surrounded by the sun, moon and stars.

Museums of Palaeontology, Ethnography, Bullfighting, Image & Sound

C/ Matías Prats, Plaza de Toros, Estepona
29680 Málaga
Tel: +34 952 80 71 48

Estepona Bull Ring is within walking distance of the town and promenade. There are four small museums here that give an insight into various aspects of Spanish history.

Admission is free and the opening hours are 10am to 2pm all year round, 4pm to 6pm in winter and 5pm to 6.30pm in summer.

The four museums are:

Museum of Ethnography: A collection of some 2,000 pieces sharing Estepona's past customs and lifestyle.

Antonio Ordóñez Museum of Bullfighting: Learn all one of Spain's most traditional sports with this fascinating collection of bullfighting memorabilia and some stunning matadors costumes.

Museum of Image and Sound: The Edgar Neville Hall has an amazing collection of projectors and cameras and in the María Isbert Hall and Spring Music Hall there are mementoes from visiting artists and their concerts.

Museum of Palaeontology: Scholars from all over Europe use the marine and mollusc collections here. There are also ten specimens of dinosaurs from Argentina and an example of a unique coral reef.

Parque San Isidro & Necropolis Visitor Centre

Los Pedregales, Estepona, 29680 Málaga

Five kilometres outside of the town set in a large country park is the reconstruction of an archaeological site.

Thanks to the construction of the new toll road at the beginning of the 21st century experts discovered several bodies and five tombs in the Estepona area. All these exciting finds were moved to Los Pedregales so everyone could see first-hand the stone beads, tools, arrow heads, axes and pottery that had been uncovered. A new visitor centre was created in the park which is also used for small concerts which are held regularly. The park has some lovely areas for walking and studying the flora and fauna as well as areas for picnics and barbeques.

Funny Beach Amusement Park

A7 Km 184
Marbella
29603 Málaga
Tel: +34 952 823 359
www.funnybeach.com

Funny Beach Amusement Park is easy to find as there is a giant inflatable Coca Cola can that sits at the entrance. There is loads of fun for all the family here, the parking is easy and it is right by the edge of the wide sandy beach. There is go-karting for adults and children as well as two-seater karts, parasailing, jet skis, banana boat rides, water skiing, trampolines and a whole host of other activities.

Food and drink is never a problem as there are three great places to choose from depending on what you fancy. For a relaxed lunch the beach bar has plenty of tables to choose from and a wide and varied menu with lots of freshly caught fish and shellfish.

The restaurant is slightly more upmarket and offers the same excellent service and quality. The beach club has luxurious sunbeds with canopies and is the place to go to be spoilt. There is a full programme of events and music on through the summer months so check on the website before you go.

Funny Beach is open 365 days a year from 11am right through until 11pm and the beach club stays open to 2am. Charges vary per activity but all the prices are clearly listed on the Funny Beach website.

Boat Trips from Marbella to Puerto Banus

www.fly-blue.com/

Get on board a water taxi and enjoy the breezy sea air on the trip between Marbella and Puerto Banús. The boats leave from the marinas of the respective towns every hour and the trip lasts for an hour. There are beautiful views along the coastline as you sail gently between the two towns passing the five star hotels on the Golden Mile and luxury mansions sprawling at the foot of La Concha. The ferry runs from 1st March until 30th November and adult single ticket is €8.50, child €5. There are slight discounts for return tickets.

For a longer sailing trip Fly Blue have a catamaran that takes you out into the Mediterranean Sea and offers chances to swim in the clear blue water and maybe see dolphins. There is a free bar for an hour while on board and opportunities to try out some water sports. The trips depart twice daily from each port and the cost is €50 for adults and €25 for children. The trip lasts for three hours.

Alcornocales Natural Park & Cortes de la Frontera

Serrania de Ronda
29380 Málaga
Tel: +34 952 15 40 00
www.cortesdelafrontera.es/

Cortes de la Frontera is a village that lays hidden deep in the forest in the Alcornocales Natural Park. The village is small but has its own train station approximately two kilometres away from the centre. Unfortunately there are not any trains from Marbella but a drive through the great expanses of uninhabited Mediterranean forests more than makes up for it. The train actually runs from La Linea near Gibraltar up to Ronda and there are several stopping points on the way. It is an excellent way of seeing the beauty that this part of Andalucía has to offer.

Cortes might only be small but like every Spanish village it has its share of festivals. In June the parade for the Virgin of the Rosary winds through the streets and there is also a fair dedicated to horses.

In August the village celebrates the fair of San Roque and San Sebastián, the towns patron saints. There are dances, contests and a cattle fair plus the release of a bull into the streets. Naturally being Spain there is a plethora of colour and sound, accompanied by lots of food and drink.

There are many places to try the local delicacies in the village and veal is a popular choice, along with locally produced hams, honey and cheese. In autumn wild boar is always on the menu for anyone wanting to try something different.

The park of Los Alcornocales spreads across the provinces of Málaga and Cadiz and covers 17 municipalities. Alcornocales means cork oak groves and it isn't hard to work out why. Cork is big business and Spain is the biggest producer of cork in the world, much of it coming from Andalucía. The men that harvest the cork spend two years training to learn their craft and the bark is cut on a nine year cycle.

Golf Courses

Andalucía is famous for its golf courses and there are almost 100 of them, with two thirds being on the Costa del Sol, or Costa del Golf as it is sometimes called. Golfing is big business and for visitors wishing to play a few rounds or get some practice in the choice is huge. Four of the courses on the Costa del Sol are in Europe's top ten including Los Naranjos in Marbella. The majority of the courses have 18 holes but there are some nine-hole courses. Green fees and buggy hire are quite reasonable and there are many companies that organise golfing packages.

Los Naranjos

Plaza Cibeles
Nueva Andalucía
29660, Marbella
Tel: +34 952 81 52 06
www.losnaranjos.com/

Los Naranjos opened in 1977 and was designed by Robert Trent Jones Sr. Many improvements have been made over the years and the course offers amateurs and professionals the chance to play a few rounds only a short putt from Puerto Banús.

Marbella Golf & Country Club

Ctra de Cádiz, N-340 Km.188
29604 Marbella
Tel: + 34 952 83 05 00
www.marbellagolf.com

Marbella Golf offers one of the most challenging courses on the coast, and is only a five minute drive from the centre of Marbella. There is a putting green, three tennis courts and a shop as well as the club house and restaurant with beautiful views across the immaculately manicured grass.

Magna Marbella Golf

Calle Calderón de la Barca
29660 Marbella
Tel. +34 952 92 92 49
www.magnamarbellagolf.com/

This is one of the regions nine-hole golf courses and was designed by José Maria Elguezabal. It is quite a demanding course with many water hazards but can be got round in less than two hours with with some very precise playing. For refreshments and a bird's eye view across the green the Millionaires Club and Restaurant will cater to your every need.

Recommendations for the Budget Traveller

Places to Stay

La Villa Marbella

Calle Principe 10, Old Historic Town, 29600 Marbella
(+34) 952 76 62 20
http://www.lavillamarbella.com/

Averaging 150€ per night, depending upon the season, La Villa Marbella is a great place to stay while visiting Marbella.

Its location is ideal with Orange Square only a three-minute walk away and Puerto Banus only a ten-minute walk. This is a romantic hotel that offers free breakfast to its guests, as well as complementary WiFi and laundry facilities. Guests can also enjoy the bar and lounge as well as the scenic rooftop terrace. There is a babysitter service as well as airport transfers.

La Morada Mas Hermosa Hotel

Calle Montenebros 16
Casco Antiguo, 29601 Marbella
+34 952 92 44 67
http://www.lamoradamashermosa.com/

La Morada Mas Hermosa is a beautiful hotel located in the Old Town of Marbella.

It is situated on a pedestrian only street, and you can park in the nearby Mercado Municipal, only a 200-meter walk from the hotel. Guests can get a breakfast basket delivered to their rooms, or take their breakfast in the common area. Rooms average 100€ per night depending on the type of room and time of year. The hotel also offers airport transfers.

Hotel-Apartamentos Puerta de Aduares

C/ Aduar, 18, 29601
Marbella
(+34) 952 82 13 12
http://www.puertadeaduares.com/

This centrally located hotel offers roomy apartment-like accommodations on a budget. Averaging 100€, the "rooms" are a steal with their kitchenettes and terraces or balconies. Parking is free. The beaches are only a five-minute walk from the hotel; which sits on a quiet, residential street. The owners are friendly as well.

Vincci Seleccion Estrella del Mar

Carretera Nacional 340 Km 191, Las Chapas, 29604
Marbella
(+34) 951 05 39 70
http://www.vinccihoteles.com

This is a resort with every amenity you can imagine averaging 150€ per night. The resort is located just besides the sea and has beach access as well as an outdoor swimming pool. It is 5 miles (8 km) from the center of Marbella in the area of Elviria Las Chapas. Its 137 rooms and suites reflect a modern Mediterranean style with a bit of Arab influence. This is the hotel to book if you are on a slight budget but want to feel like high society.

Princesa Playa Hotel Apartamentos

Paseo Maritimo, s/n, 29600 Marbella
(+34) 952 82 09 44
http://www.hotelprincesaplaya.com/en/index.htm

The Princesa Playa Hotel Apartamentos is a value,
averaging 75€ per night and located right on the beach
with only a five-minute walk to the Old Town. It offers 64
rooms and 36 apartments as well as a restaurant, a terrace
bar and outdoors swimming pool. It was completely
refurbished in 2006, but is still an older hotel; so if you are
looking for something very modern, you might want to
consider looking elsewhere. Still, it is a great value and
spotlessly clean.

Eating & Drinking

Tempora

Tetuan 9a
29601 Marbella
(+34) 95 285 7933

Tempora is a newer restaurant in the Old Town of
Marbella with a name that means, "season" in Spanish.

Despite its youth, this quaint establishment has already garnered the respect and adoration of both locals and tourists alike. The owner's philosophy is to cook with fresh, seasonal ingredients in order to prepare and serve dishes of the highest possible quality.

Every day, Chef Abraham Garrote Costa accompanies owner, Andrés Perdiguero to the local market in search for the ingredients that will suit their menu for the day. Since they use only the produce that is "in season," you will most likely find a different menu with each visit. To find the restaurant, find the horse fountain across from Parque de Alameda. Once at the fountain, Tetuan is the first street on your right. Tempora is on the left side of the street, in the middle of the block.

Expect to pay an average of 20€ per entrée. Reservations are accepted.

Rendez Vous

Avenida del Prado Nueva Andalucia
29660 Marbella
(+34) 952 813 912
http://rendezvous-marbella.com/

Rendez Vous is a French bistro located in the heart of Marbella. The owners, Mikael and Céline, are known for their traditional French dishes and their macarons. Do not be intimidated by its fancy interior.

It is budget friendly while classy. Rendez Vous is open on Tuesdays through Sundays from 9 a.m. until 5 p.m. for breakfast and lunch. On Sundays, they offer a brunch service. Every Friday, from 7 p.m. until 9 p.m., the restaurant offers champagne tasting paired with some of Chef Mikael's dishes.

Stuzzikini

c/ Alderete 5,
29600 Marbella
(+34) 952 775 994
http://www.stuzzikini.com/

Stuzzikini is the project of Chef Robert, who has spent his formative cooking years in Italy, Spain, and England. He serves Italian food that makes people think they are in Sardinia. The dishes are unique but still carry a trace of their homelands. Atmosphere at Stuzzikini is relaxed but adheres to a high attention to detail that includes charming Italian music. Stuzzikini is open daily except for Tuesdays, from 7:00 p.m. until close. Reservations are recommended.

La Taberna del Pintxo

Avenida Miguel Cano 7, 29600 Marbella
(+34) 952 829 321
http://www.latabernadelpintxo.com/

The Basque regions equivalent of "tapas" is a "pinxto," which is this Basque restaurants specialty. La Taberna del Pintxo offer two categories of pinxtos - cold and hot.

The cold pinxtos can be purchased at the bar while the hot pinxtos are served at the table. The cuisine includes flavors from both the north and south of Spain as well as ingredients of the best quality. They are also known for serving good Spanish wine.

Bar El Estrecho

Calle San Lazaro 12
Old Town, 29601 Marbella
(+34) 95 277 0004
http://www.barelestrecho.es/

Open since 1954, this tapas restaurant serves traditional Spanish cuisine in a charming atmosphere. It is slightly hidden, in a narrow alley in old town, but this should not discourage you from looking for it. Service is consistently friendly and accommodating. Prices range from $5 to $15.

Shopping

Considering the fact that Marbella is one of those destinations where people go to see and be seen, one of the most popular things to shop for is clothing. Although it has its share of high-end shops, Marbella also offers its visitors fashionable European style apparel at more reasonable prices than in many other European cities.

If you are looking for something in particular, Marbella's megastores like El Corte Ingles will not disappoint. But the best way to find hidden treasures at bargain prices is simply to stroll through town and stop at one of the many local merchants or street markets.

Puerto Banus Street Market

Boulevard de La Fama
(Parking is at Centro Plaza mall on Calle Camilo Jose Cela)

Just a short walk from the centre of Puerto Banus and located near the bullring is the Saturday Puerto Banus street market. This is a great place to buy souvenirs and just about anything else you can imagine. Start at the bullring and head down to the port as you browse the spices, clothes, vegetables, and furniture. Parking can be congested, so be sure to arrive early or late. Although it opens at 9 a.m., many stalls aren't ready until 10 a.m. It closes at 2 p.m.

El Corte Ingles

Calle Ramón Areces
Puerto Banus
(+34) 952 909 990
http://www.elcorteingles.es/

El Corte Inglés is the major department store in Marbella and is the largest shopping chain in Spain and all of Europe. It is here that you can find everything you need, including brands from the best names in fashion. There is also a supermarket (Hipercor), optician, and travel agency.

El Corte Ingles is open Monday through Saturday from 10:00 a.m. to 10:00 p.m. in the winter and daily from 10:30 a.m. to 10:30 p.m. in the summer.

Marina Banus

Calle Ramon Areces, 29600
(+34) 952 906 544
http://www.marinabanus.com/

If El Corte Ingles is too overwhelming for you, Marina Banus may be more your style.

Simply head across the road from El Corte Ingles to reach this smaller, budget-friendly mall. Within the mall are approximately 30 stores as well as restaurants and a hair salon. It is also family-friendly with a play area for toddlers. The mall is open Monday through Saturday from 10:00 a.m. to 10:00 p.m. in the winter and daily from 10:30 a.m. to 10:30 p.m. in the summer.

Centro Comercial La Cañada

Carretera Ojén, Marbella 29602
(+34) 95 286 5076

The Centro Comercial La Cañada is similar to Marina Banus in size and has everything you would expect from a mall. The difference is mostly in its ample parking spaces and that it is less crowded than the malls on Puerto Banus. The shops include Armand Basi, Mango, Zara, and Dorothy Perkins and there is a large Alcampo supermarket. The Centro Comercial La Cañada is open daily from 10 a.m. until 10 p.m. (except Sundays).

Zoco del Sol Market

Plaza Antonio Banderas,
Puerto Banus

The Zoco del Sol is an open-air market that occurs daily during the summertime. During the rest of the year, it is open only on Saturdays. Situated on Plaza Antonio Banderas (named after the famous movie actor who was born in the area) between the El Corte Ingles Shopping Center and the port, this market has 25 stalls that sell unique art, vintage clothing, jewelry, fragrances, and glass. Park in the lot under the central square and walk the short distance to the market. It is open from 11 a.m. until midnight during the summer and from 10 a.m. until 4 p.m. on Saturdays during the rest of the year.

43106293R00029

Made in the USA
Middletown, DE
30 April 2017